This book belongs to

Name:

AGE:

Address:

Email:

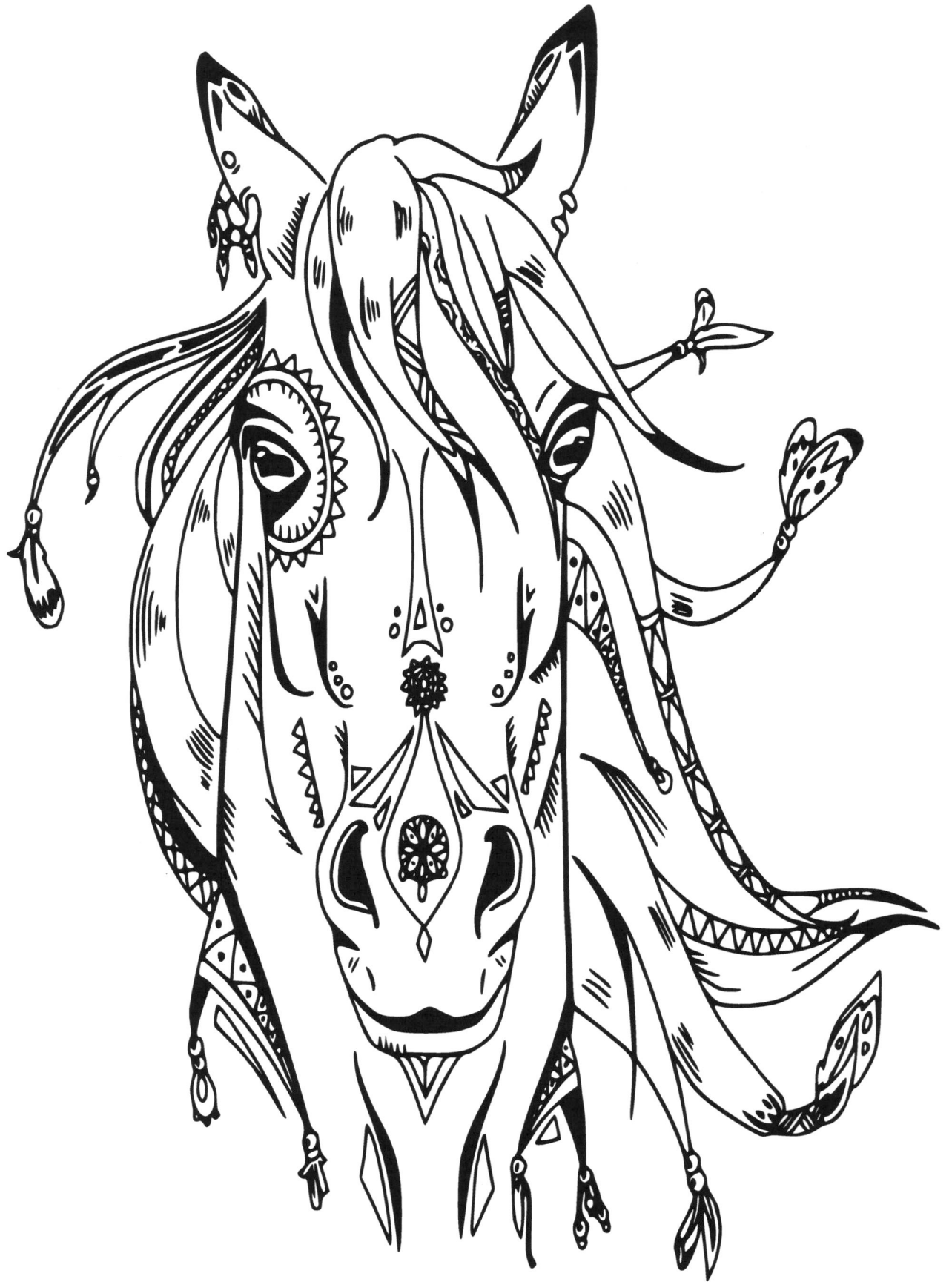

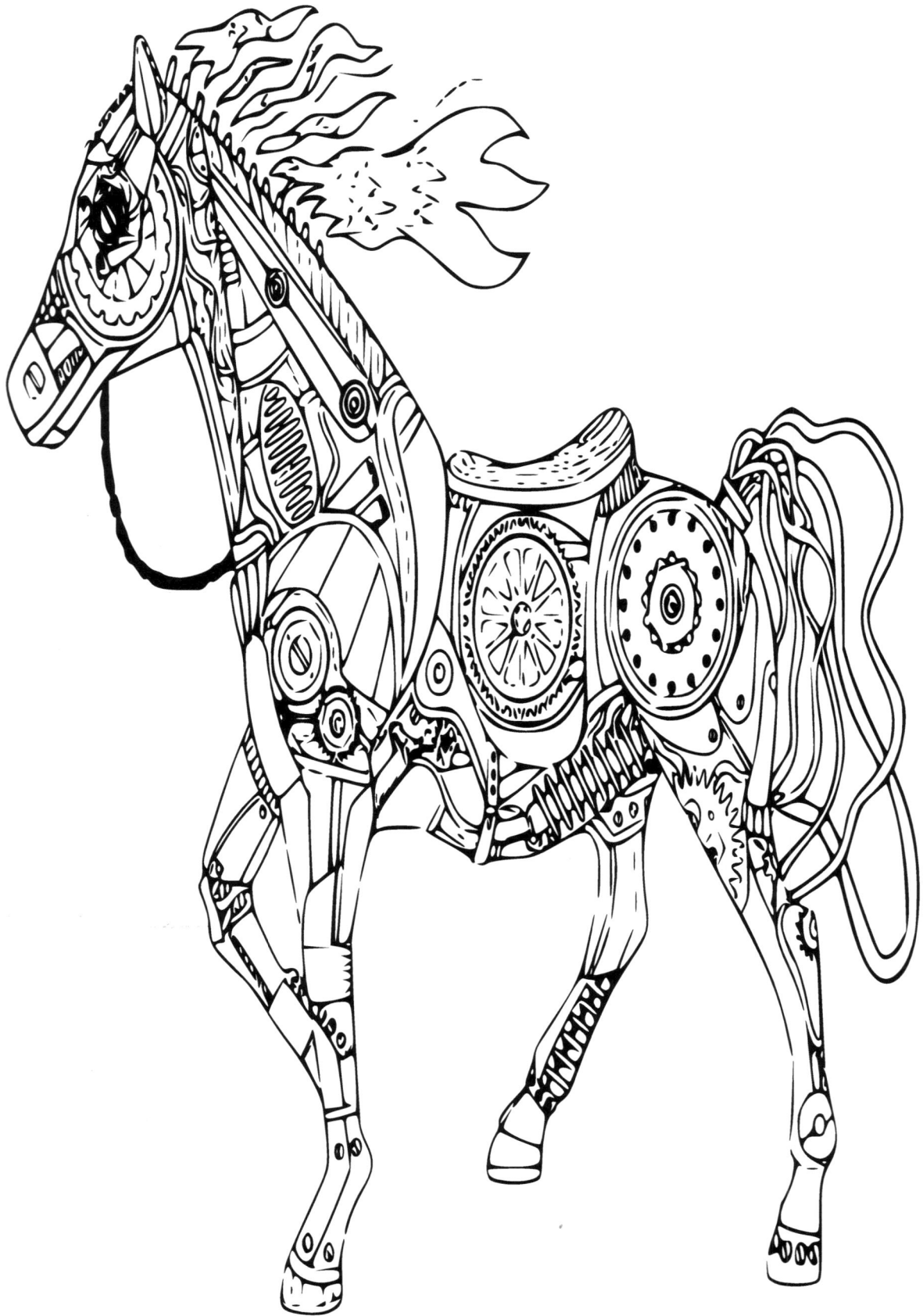

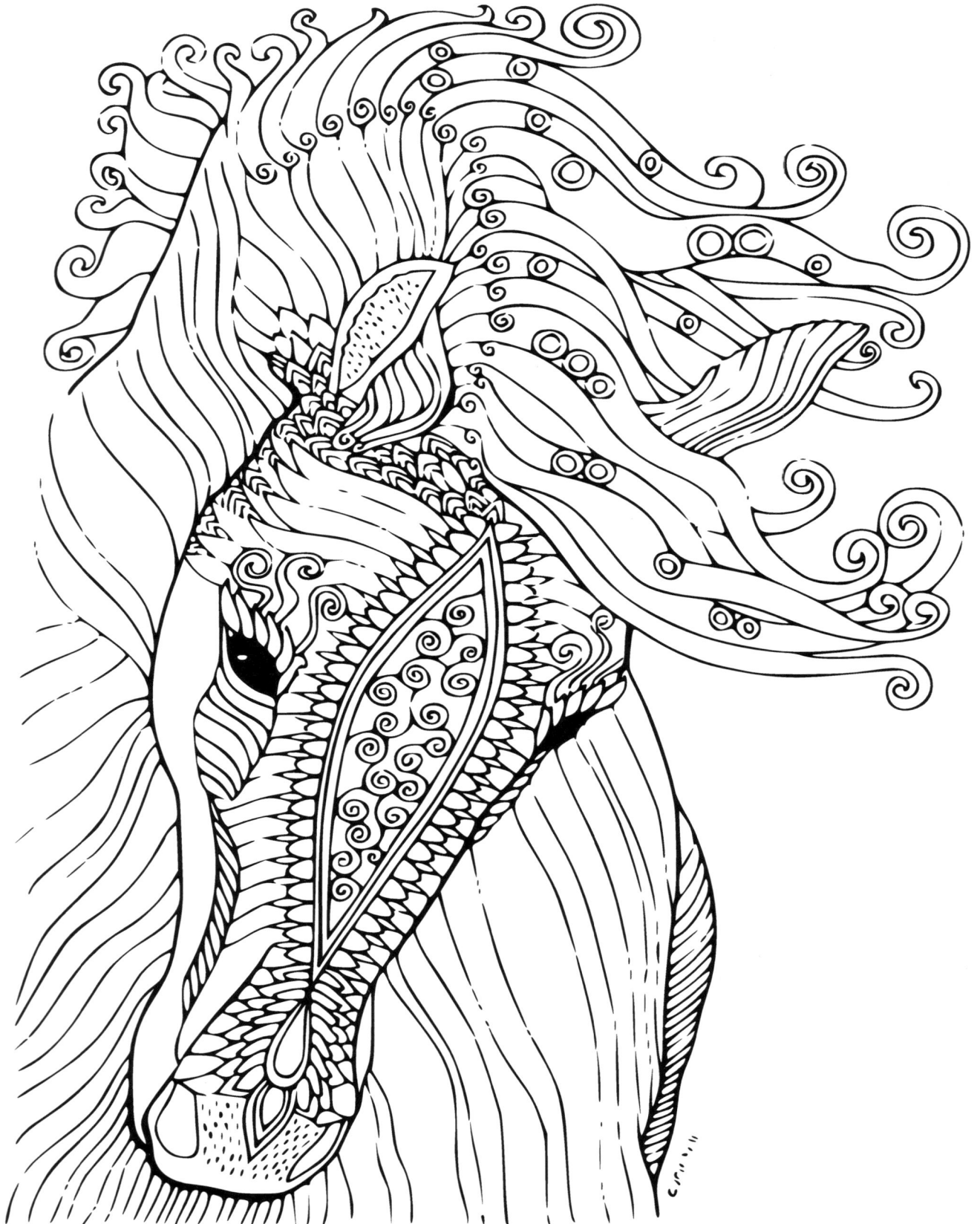

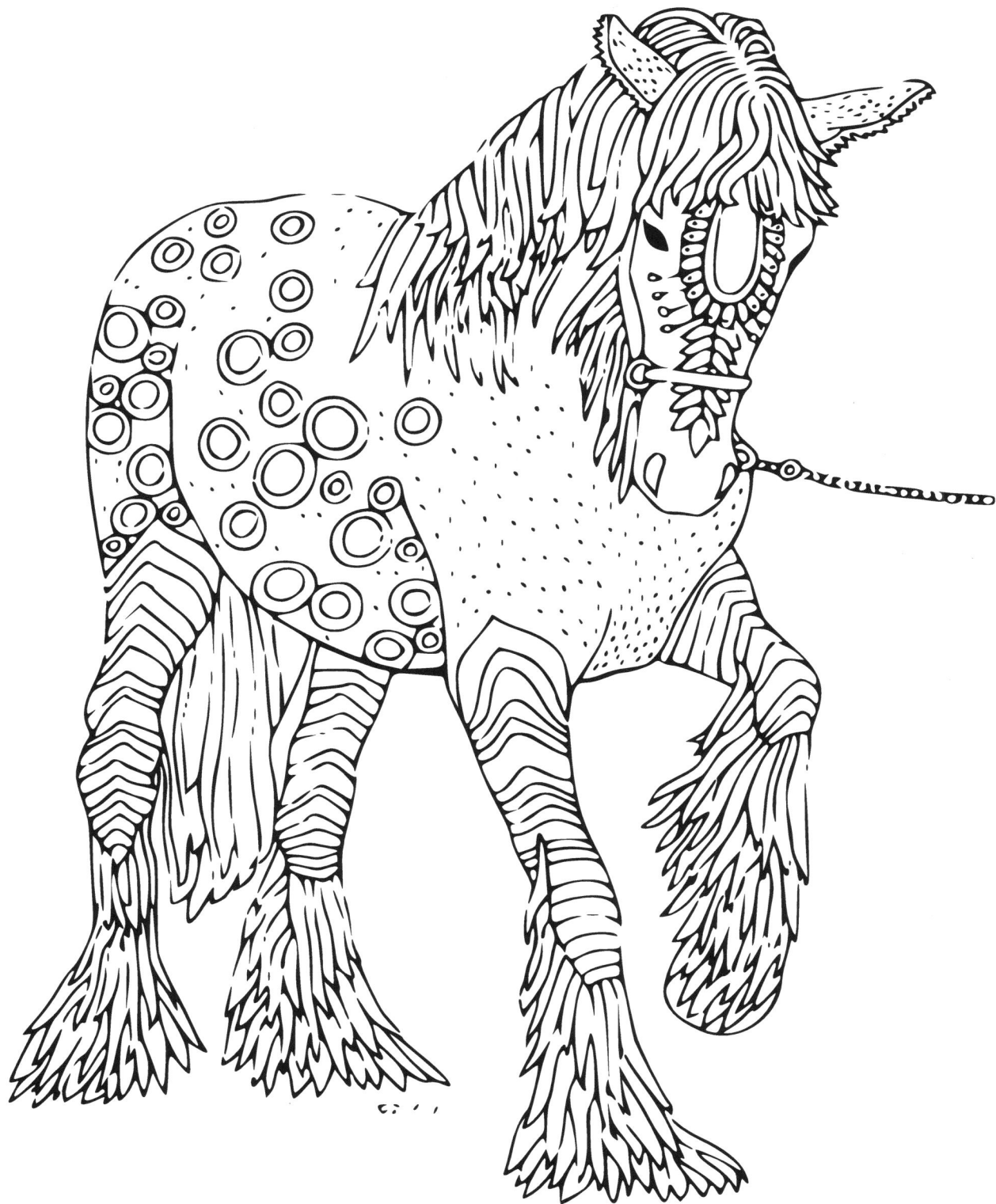

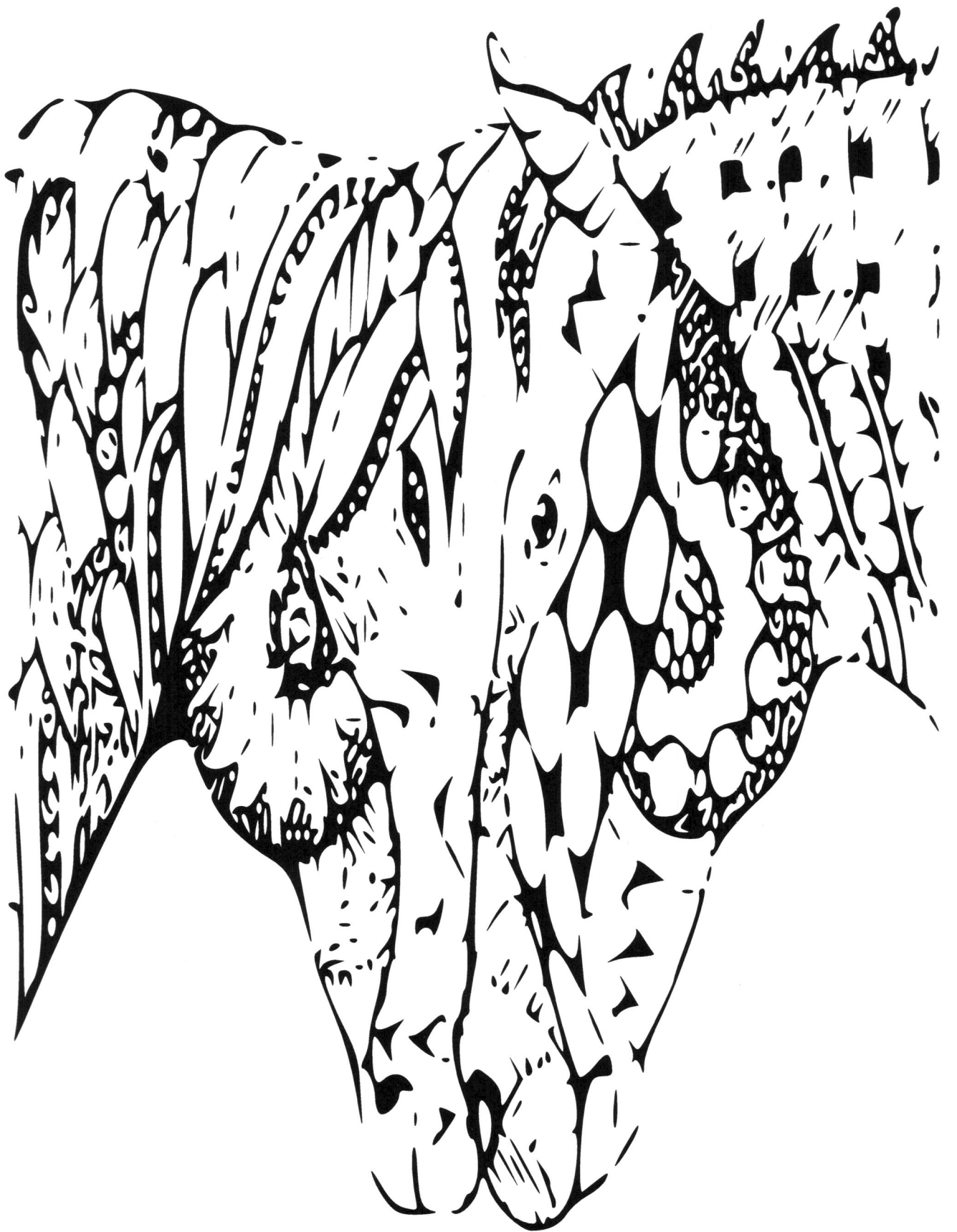

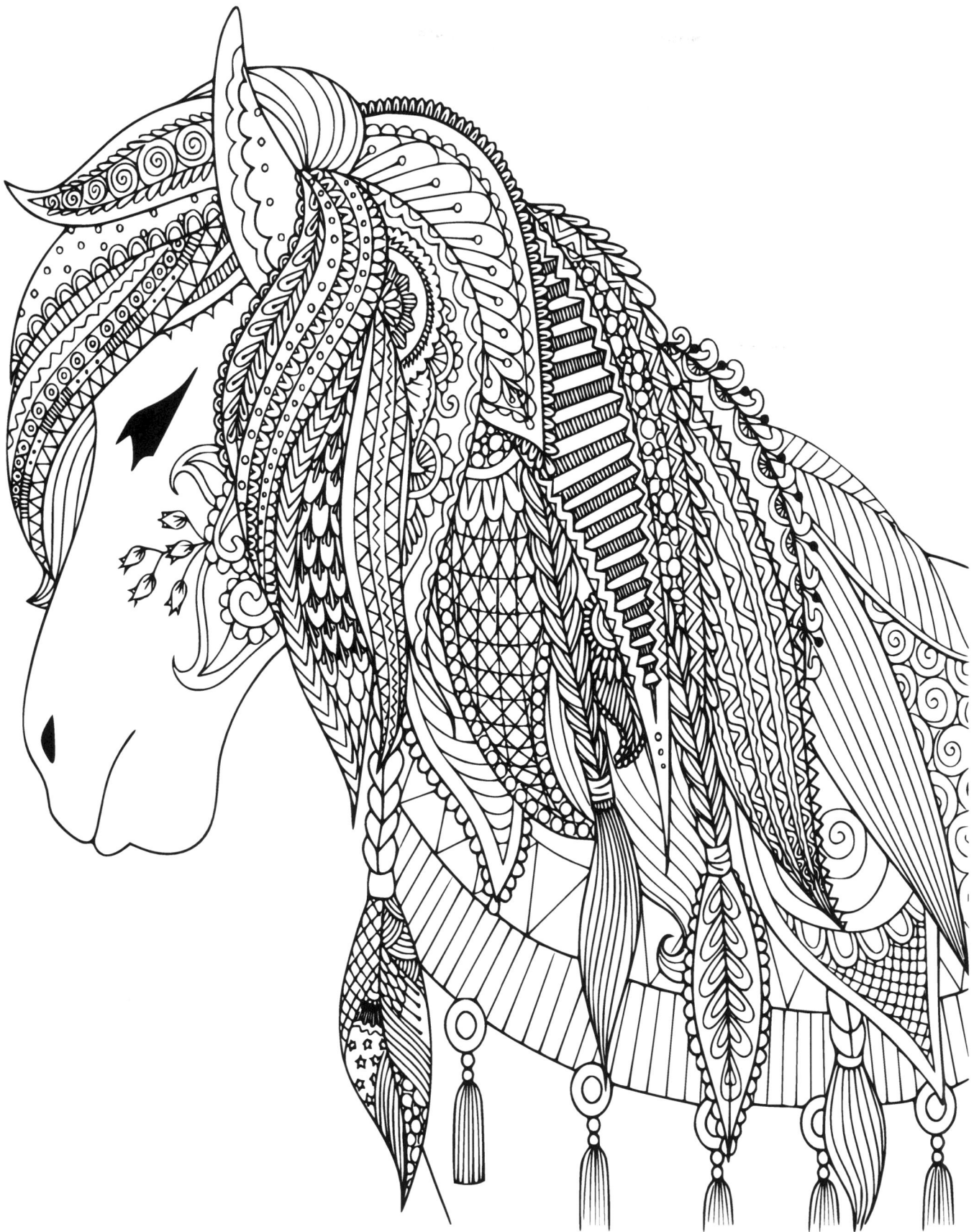

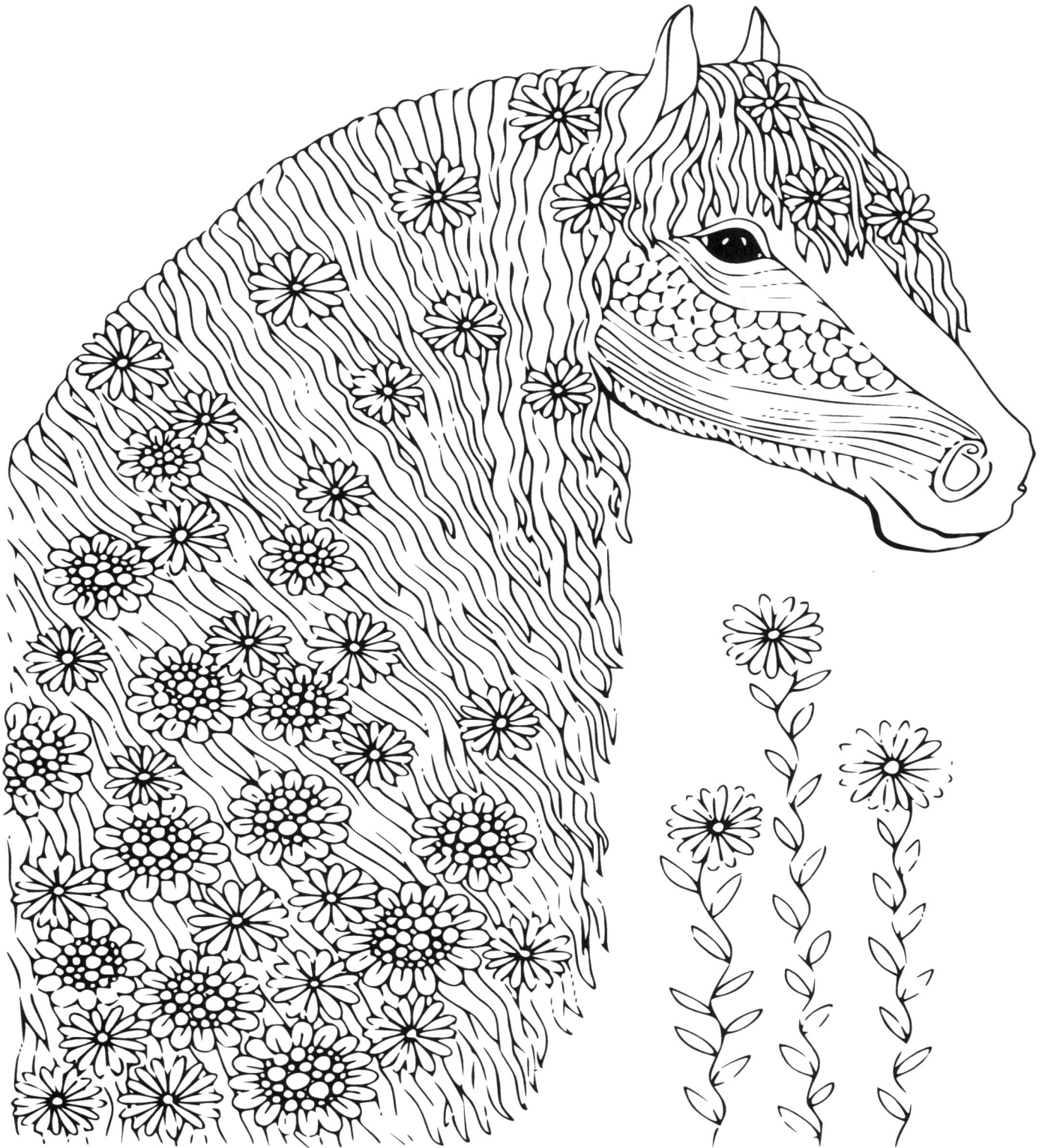

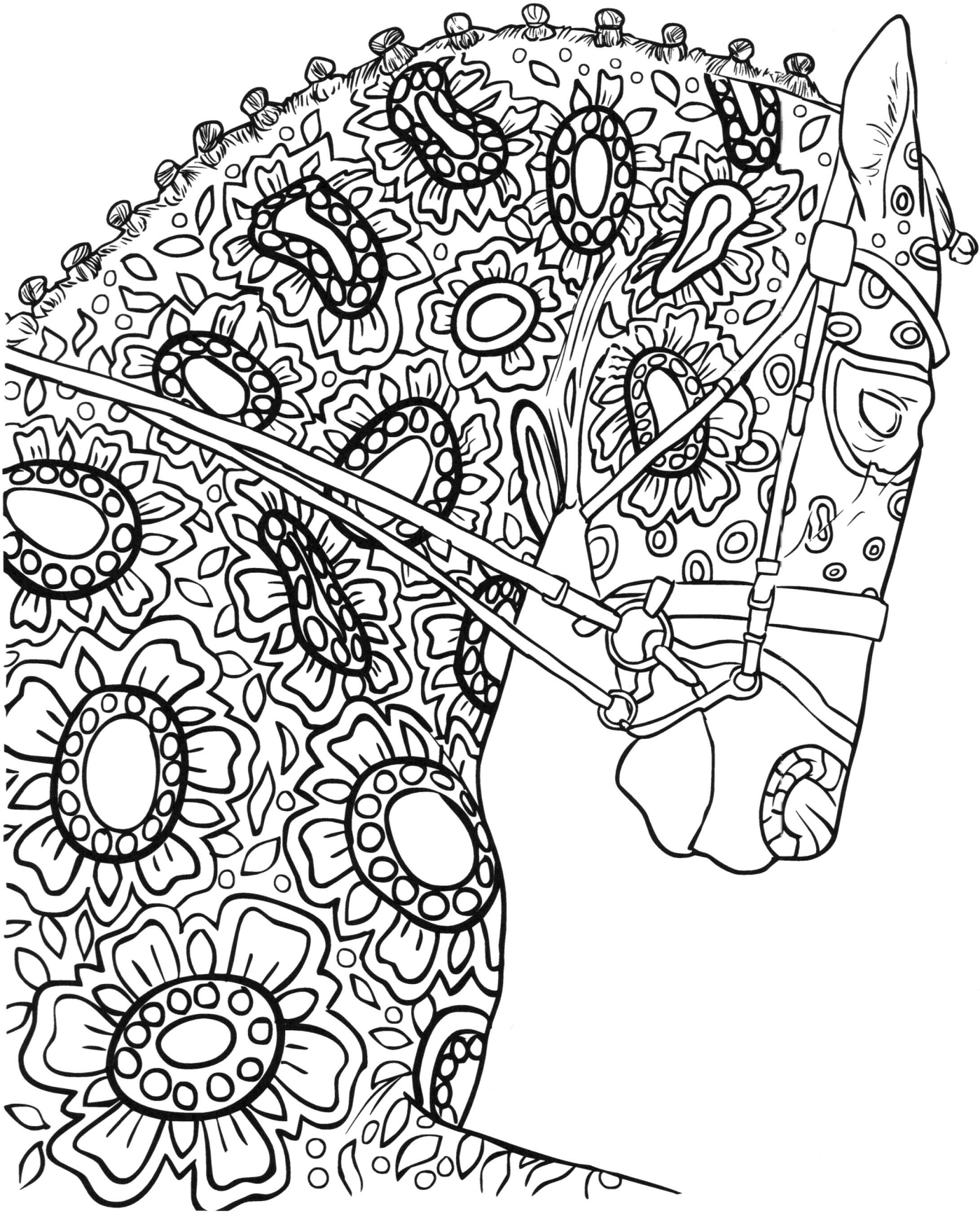

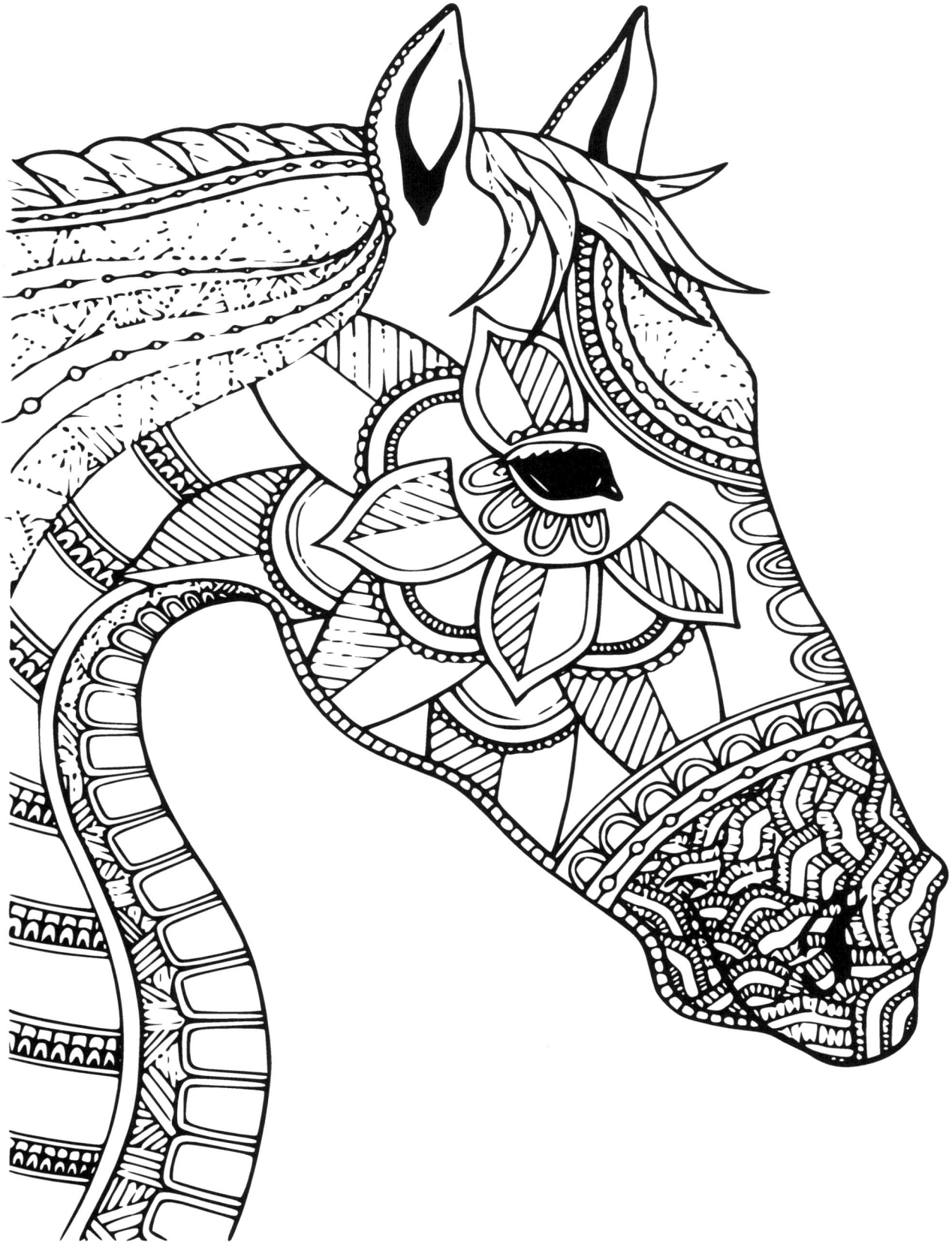

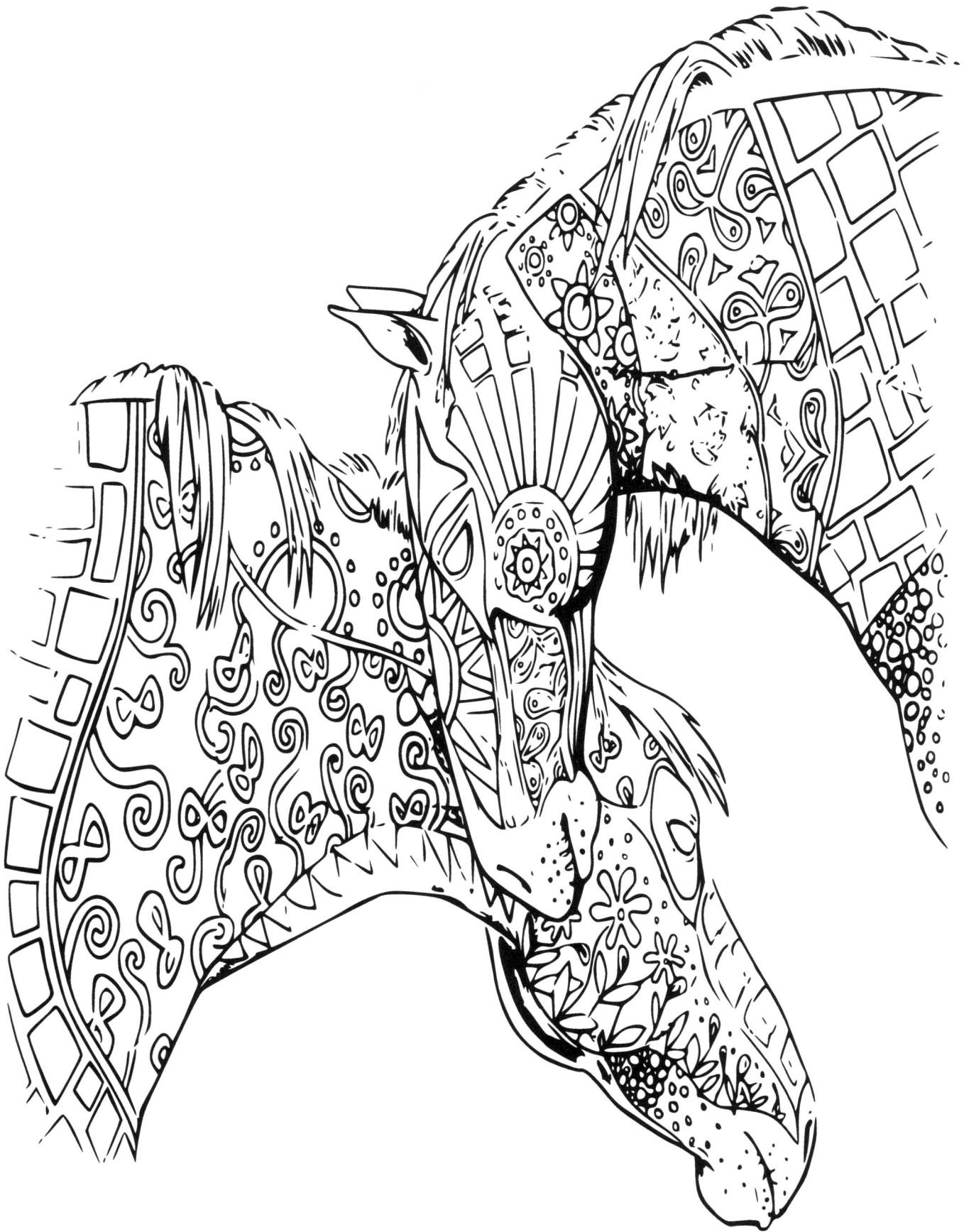

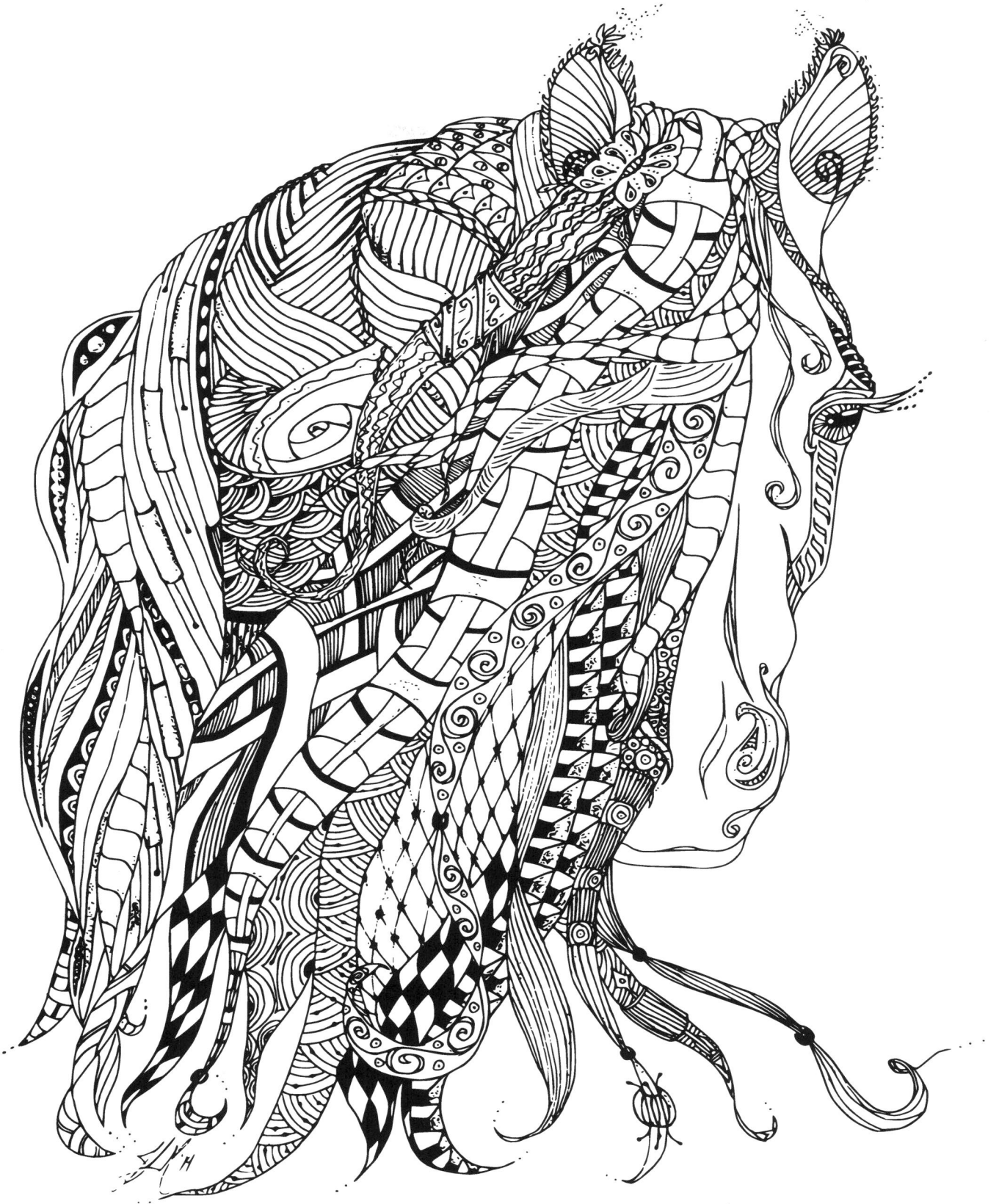

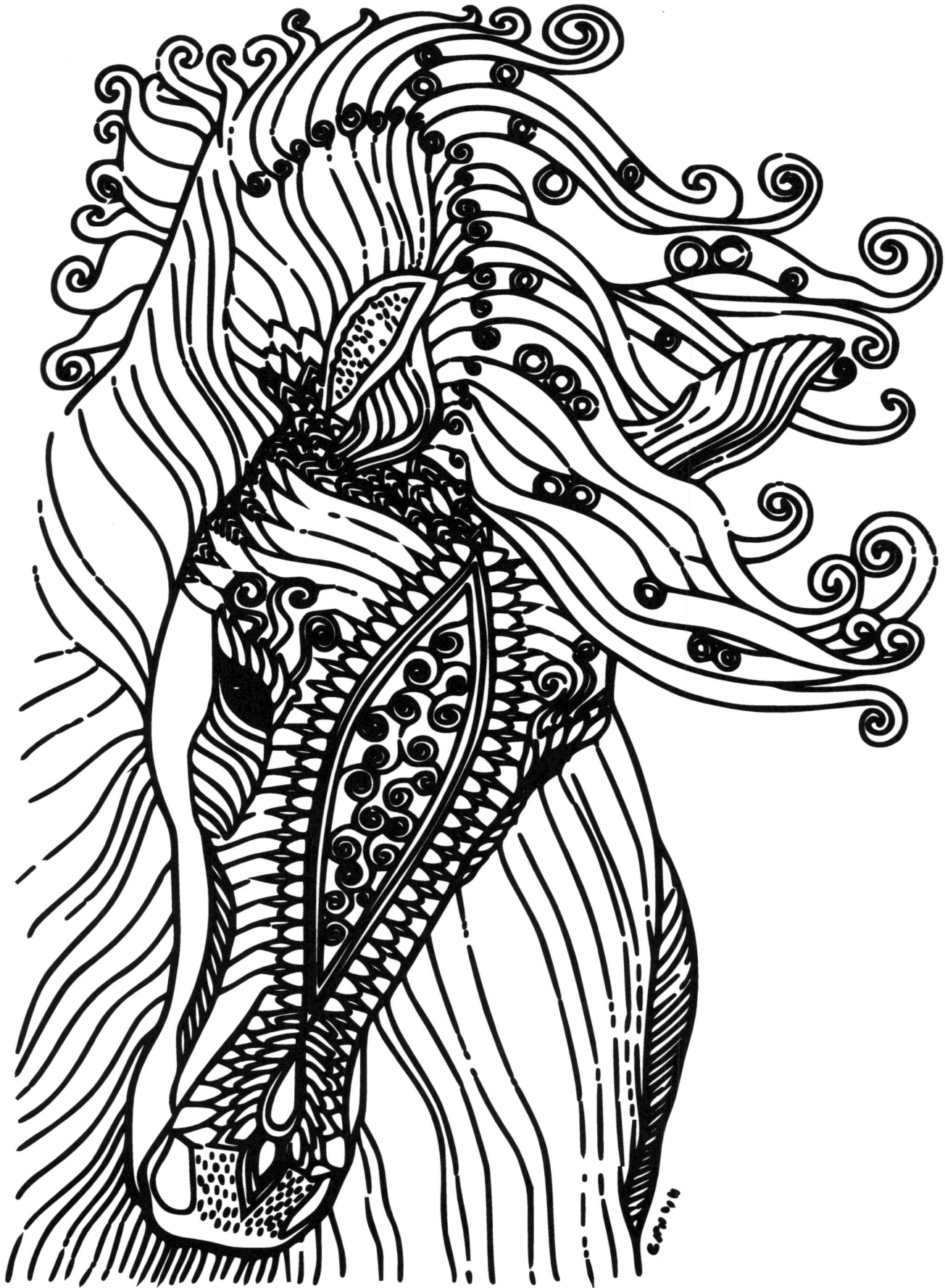

DEAR CUSTOMER

THANKS FOR SHOPPING WITH US!

WE HOPE YOU'RE ENJOYING YOUR PURCHASE

WE'D LIKE TO ASK FOR FAVOR-COULD YOU SHARE

YOUR BUYING EXPERIENCE WITH US?

IT WILL TAKE YOU ABOUT 4 MUNITES TO COMPLETE

OUR SURVEY,BUT IT'LL BE INVALUABLE TO US FOR
IMPROVING OUR SERVICES

THANKS!